For my mother, Eilene Maret, Ph.D., whose life work in the field of social emotional learning serves as inspiration for the Emotional Wellness Project™ and this book.

www.mascotbooks.com

My Incredible Talking Body: Learning to Be Calm

For more information, please contact:
Mascot Books
560 Herndon Parkway #120
Herndon, VA 20170
info@mascotbooks.com

Library of Congress Control Number: 2017900392

CPSIA Code: PRT0217A
ISBN-13: 978-0-99719-62-0-7

Printed in the United States

My Incredible Talking Body

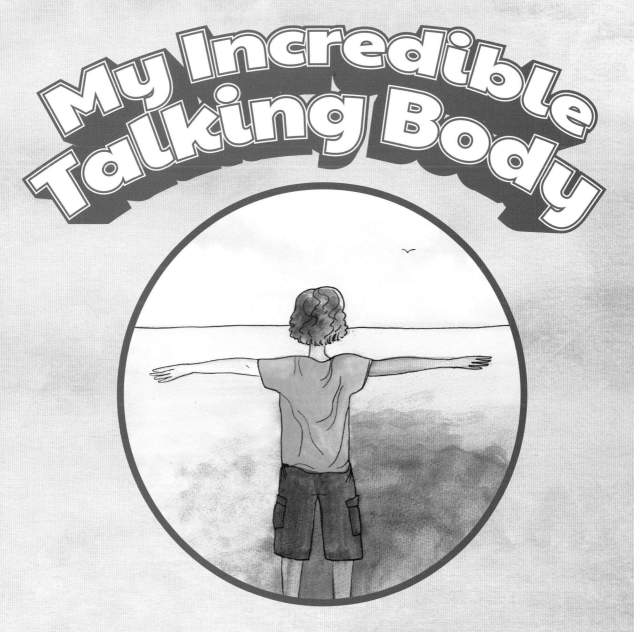

Learning to Be Calm

by Rebecca Bowen • illustrated by Lauren Bowen

The Emotional Wellness Project
www.EmotionalWellnessProject.com

When I listen closely,
my body **talks** to me.

It tells me I am **hungry** when my stomach feels empty and makes rumbly noises.

It tells me I am **thirsty** when my mouth is dry and I really want to get a drink of water.

It tells me I am **sleepy** when my eyes are droopy and I just can't stop yawning.

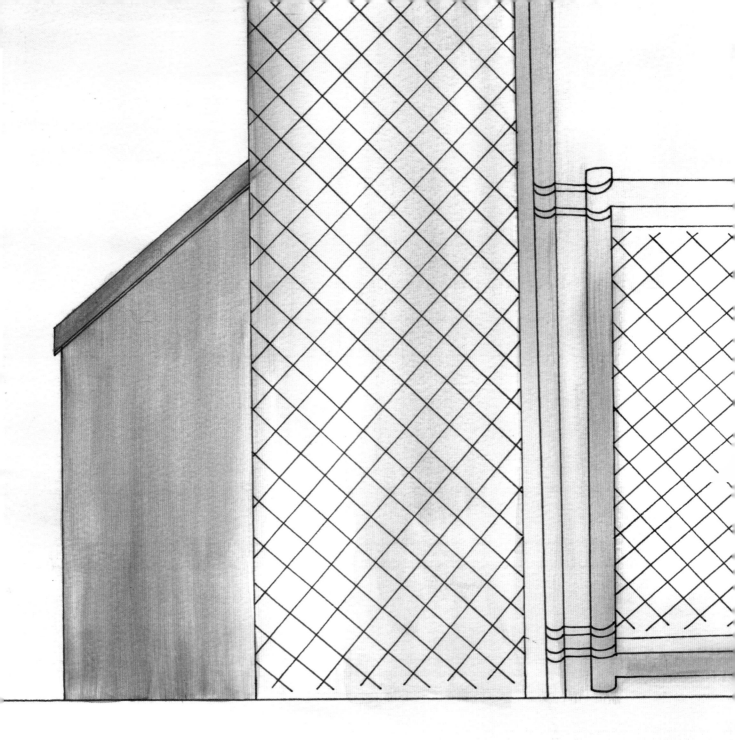

My body also talks to me about my **feelings.**

When I am **angry,** my muscles get tight. My breathing is fast and growly like a bear. Sometimes my face gets really hot and turns red like a tomato. It is hard to think when I am angry.

When I am **sad,** my body feels heavy like I'm carrying an elephant in my backpack. My face feels hot and wet. It is hard to breathe when I am crying, and even harder to talk. I don't feel like playing when I'm really sad. I don't feel like doing anything.

When I am **scared,** it feels like
I'm being chased by a cheetah.
My heart beats really fast.
My breathing gets all messed up
and sometimes...
I forget to breathe at all.

When I am **calm,** my muscles feel relaxed like my arms and legs have turned into spaghetti noodles.

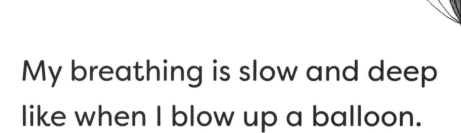

My breathing is slow and deep like when I blow up a balloon.

My brain thinks about butterflies and bunny rabbits and things that make me smile.

All of my feelings are okay. It is okay to be **angry.** But it is not okay to break things or hurt somebody... anybody... even myself.

It is okay to be **sad.** But it is not okay to say mean words that hurt somebody's feelings, or lie down on the floor and not get up.

It is okay to be **scared.** But sometimes I have to try really hard to do what I am supposed to do even when it's scary.

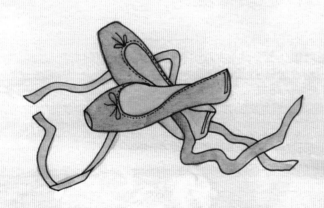

When I have a really strong feeling, I can do something to help myself get **calm** again.

I can take deep breaths, tell myself, "calm down," or count very slowly.

I can spend time alone reading a book,

drawing a picture,
or putting together
my favorite puzzle.

I can talk to somebody I trust

or hug my favorite stuffed animal.

or run around the playground six times.

I can lie on my bed and take a pretend vacation in my head to Hawaii, where I sit on the beach listening to the waves and watching the sun shine through the palm trees.

ALL of my feelings are okay.

But it feels much better
when I am **calm** again.

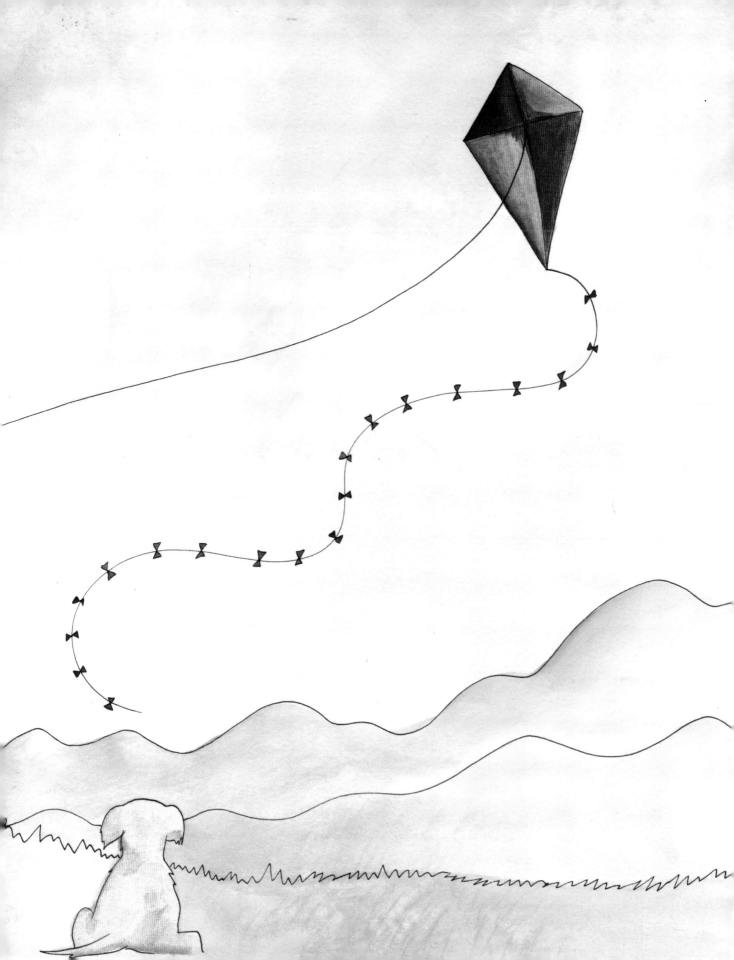

Learning Guide

A Note for Parents, Educators, and Other Grown-ups Committed to Helping Children Develop Emotional Wellness:

My Incredible Talking Body: Learning to Be Calm is a tool for becoming mindful of the body's signals about feelings, encouraging acceptance of emotions, and developing strategies for calming down from strong or uncomfortable feelings. It is designed to be read interactively to engage children in exploring the ideas and strategies with a supportive adult.

Our incredible bodies talk to us by providing important signals to keep us healthy. Just as they tell us when we need to eat, drink, or sleep to stay physically healthy, our bodies also give us important information about what we need to be emotionally well. Intense emotions such as anger and anxiety often trigger a strong response causing tight muscles, racing hearts, and fast breathing. Sadness may trigger the release of brain chemicals that result in feelings of heaviness. Unchecked, these signals may lead to stomach aches, headaches, and other physical symptoms that leave a child feeling sick or worn out.

Without the tools to calm down, children may get stuck in their feelings, becoming afraid to go to school or withdrawing from favorite activities, or they may act out emotions with unwanted behaviors. When children learn to listen to their bodies for signals about feelings, they are empowered to self-regulate by using calming strategies and as a result, they are able to retain more control over their behavior.

Encourage children to accept their feelings. Emotions are neither good nor bad and the child is neither good nor bad for having a certain feeling. This concept releases the child to simply experience an emotion while maintaining the ability to choose behavior. When ready, the child can choose to do something to calm down again.

Teaching Suggestions

- Where in your body do you feel it when you are hungry, thirsty, or sleepy? (Ask each as you come to the relevant page.)

- What is your body telling you when your tummy rumbles? When your throat is dry? When your eyelids are heavy?

- What is your body telling you to do when you feel that way?

- What could happen if you don't listen to your body's signals about being hungry, thirsty, or sleepy?

- Where in your body do you feel it when you are angry, sad, or scared?

- Show me what you look like when you feel angry, sad, or scared. (Adults, demonstrate what you look like, too! Point out the child's tight muscles, scrunched up face, or droopy arms.)

- What does your breathing sound like when you are angry, sad, or scared?

- What happens in your body when you are calm? What does calm feel like to you?

- Try the following together with the child: Wiggle your arms and legs. Pretend they have turned into spaghetti noodles. For older children use the words, "shake it off."

- Blow up a balloon. (Cup your hands together in front of your mouth and pretend to blow up a balloon by making the space between your cupped hands grow with each breath.)

- Now with bodies calm, practice getting your brain calm. Close your eyes. What makes you smile? Paint a picture of it in your mind. Describe it.

Strategies for Calming Down

- Take slow, deep breaths. Breathe in through the nose and out through the mouth. Let the tummy expand when you breathe in and relax when you breathe out.

- Use positive self-talk by saying things like, "Calm down," "I'm okay," or, "It will be alright."

- Count very slowly.

- Designate a quiet space where the child can go to calm down, not as a time out for discipline, but as a quiet place for managing feelings.

- Limit noise, lower lights, and reduce other sensory input (including talking) when emotions are strong.

- Allow calm activities like reading, drawing, or playing with puzzles to engage the creative centers of the child's brain.

- Allow children to self-soothe with sensory input such as hugging a blanket or stuffed animal, or squeezing a "stress" ball.

- Encourage exercise to help de-escalate after an intense emotional incident.

- Help children tap into the power of their thoughts to change their emotions through visualization and positive thinking.

- Provide opportunities for children to talk about feelings. Encourage them to label their feelings. Affirm that it is okay to have that feeling and help them to choose a strategy to calm down.

Additional Activities

"WHEN I LISTEN CLOSELY MY BODY TALKS TO ME!"

- Act out a variety of feelings, pointing out clues on the face and body.
- Use handheld mirrors for children to observe their own expressions.
- Play feelings charades.
- Discuss the importance of listening to the body's signals and create moments of reflection on how various body parts are feeling.
- Use a simple body outline and colored markers for children to label where various emotions are felt in their bodies.

"ALL OF MY FEELINGS ARE OKAY!"

- Point out pictures in books and situations in movies or television depicting children and adults dealing with strong emotions. Discuss how the subjects manage their feelings. Do they use healthy strategies or are their responses unhealthy? Do their reactions create a problem?
- Try talking about "comfortable" and "uncomfortable" feelings rather than labeling emotions as "bad" or using terms such as "anger problem." It is often our behavior, not the emotion itself that is the problem!
- Encourage children to label their feelings and model this by naming your own emotions.

"WHEN I HAVE A REALLY STRONG FEELING, I CAN DO SOMETHING TO HELP MYSELF GET CALM AGAIN."

- Introduce a variety of breathing strategies and guide children to pick a favorite.

- Along with the child, show how you breathe when you are sad, mad, and angry. Practice slowing down to take deep breaths.

- Upper elementary children are often interested in more details about how the body works. Research together to learn more about the mechanics of breathing and how the brain is activated by emotions.

- Practice slow, deep breaths and build body awareness with short sessions of focused breathing combined with calming music or guided voice instruction.

- Teach children to use physical activity as a strategy for calming strong emotions. Create a plan with a child and identify where they can safely run, walk, jump, or dance.

- Explore sensory experiences and, based on individual preferences, create a "calm down box" containing objects for self-soothing. Consider sights, smells, sounds, tastes, and touches that help the child feel calm.

- Engage in activities such as drawing, reading, building with toys, or doing other creative thinking tasks to stimulate a child's brain and regulate emotions.

- Teach children that they can exercise control over their thought worlds by creating fun or calm images in their minds. Play imagination games to build a bank of ideas.

- Draw pictures of happy thoughts to refer to when uncomfortable emotions linger.

- Guide a child in building a list of positive self-talk statements to address frequent emotion triggers.

For more information please visit:
www.EmotionalWellnessProject.com

Author: Rebecca Bowen

Rebecca Bowen, M.Ed. has worked for over 25 years in public schools as a special education teacher, school psychologist, and school counselor. She is deeply committed to developing emotional wellness in children and equipping educators and parents to support this growth. With her own three children grown and married, she has launched The Emotional Wellness Project™ in order to share helpful tools and resources discovered along the way. Cultivating her own emotional wellness, Rebecca is active in her faith and enjoys photography, gardening, playing the violin, and long walks with her husband along the shores of the Pacific Ocean. Visit www.EmotionalWellnessProject.com for more information.

Illustrator: Lauren Bowen

Lauren Bowen is a freelance writer passionate about branding, global issues, and the world's little mysteries. A Pacific Northwest native and Wyoming resident, Lauren can be found hiking the great outdoors, supporting nonprofit founders in their ventures, or illustrating children's books. Find out more about Lauren at www.lauren-bowen.com.